Anita Khuttan

# Everything's

## DIFFERENT BUT

## THE

## SAME

*Everything's*
DIFFERENT BUT
THE
SAME

AuthorHouse™
1663 Liberty Drive
Bloomington, IN 47403
www.authorhouse.com
Phone: 833-262-8899

Because of the dynamic nature of the Internet, any web addresses or links contained in this book may have changed
since publication and may no longer be valid. The views expressed in this work are solely those of the author and do
not necessarily reflect the views of the publisher, and the publisher hereby disclaims any responsibility for them.

Any people depicted in stock imagery provided by Getty Images are models,
and such images are being used for illustrative purposes only.
Certain stock imagery © Getty Images.

This book is printed on acid-free paper.

Interior Image Credit: Anita Khuttan

ISBN: 978-1-6655-0746-2 (sc)
978-1-6655-0747-9 (e)

Library of Congress Control Number: 2020922341

Print information available on the last page.

Published by AuthorHouse  11/28/2020

authorHOUSE®

# Anita Khuttan

# Everything's
## DIFFERENT BUT THE SAME

Cover Art Credit:
*Anita Khuttan*

Mummy doesn't take me into my class anymore.

She tells me she loves me and leaves me at the door.

Everything's different but the same.

I can't sit next to my friends as before,

2 meters distance or more,

Everything's different but the same.

We build with Lego, play games of catch and throw,

The playground has become a place we can no longer go.

Everything's different but the same.

We shout and play and draw and sing,

But cleaning hands is now a thing.

Everythings different but the same.

We used to hug but now we wave,

Smiling under our mask is how we behave.

Everything's different but the same.

We touched and played and passed our toys

Now we're wise we sanitise.

Everything's different but the same.

Home time comes and we wave goodbye,

I'll see you tomorrow, we smile with our eyes.

Our actions are different, but our feelings are the same.

Everything's different but the same.

Printed in the United States
By Bookmasters